The View Ever Changing

The View Ever Changing

Poems by

Karen Luke Jackson

Cover art: Compilation by Jonathan Royal Jackson
of window photo by John-Mark Smith on Unsplash
and night sky by Karen Luke Jackson

Cover design by Shay Culligan

Back cover headshot by Erica Mueller

ISBN: 978-1-954353-22-0

Also by Karen Luke Jackson "GRIT"

Kelsay Books
502 South 1040 East, A-119
American Fork, Utah, 84003

For Jackson, Kaia, and Auden
and the generations who may follow.

Acknowledgments

Many thanks to teachers Ken Chamlee, Cathy Smith Bowers, Janisse Ray, Eric Nelson, Pat Riviere-Seel, and Tina Barr. Also, to fellow writers who have critiqued my work and accompanied me on this journey: Anne Westbrook Green, Jane Curran, Emily Wilmer, Kathleen Calby, Kathy Nelson, Tonya Staufer, Jennifer McGaha, and Rebecca Ethridge.

Also, immense gratitude to my son, Jonathan Royal Jackson, for the compilation photograph that graces the book's cover, and to my daughter, Kerri, who shares my love of books.

Grateful acknowledgment is made to the following publications in which some of the poems in this collection first appeared.

The Blue Mountain Review: "Stomping Grounds"
Broad River Review: "A Triptych on the First Anniversary of My Mother's Death," Winner of the Ron Rash Poetry Prize, 2012
Channel Magazine: "Homage to the Least"
The Great Smokies Review: "Hopscotch," "Home Movies," and "Heading for Home"
GRIT (Finishing Line Press, 2020): "Sisters: Take Two"
Kakalak: "Snapper Head Bait & Tackle," "Steady Walkers," "Bobwhites," "Hooked," and "Amends" (now "Prodigal")
Kestrel: "Application"
Leaping Clear: "Elegy for My Childhood Trees," "Breakers" (now "Learning to Float"), "Night View from a Bedroom Window" and "Living Room"
One: "Deconstructing Goldilocks"
Redheaded Stepchild: "Prayer for a Dying Father"
Untold Volumes, Christian Feminism Today: "Glenmary Sister"

"Rite of Passage" (now "True Believers") was awarded Honorable Mention, and "Deconstructing Goldilocks" was awarded First Place in the Sidney Lanier Library Poetry Contest, 2017.

Contents

III. Gravity

IV. Coming Down through the Women's Line

V. What We Do to Earth

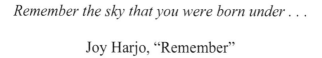

Remember the sky that you were born under . . .

Joy Harjo, "Remember"

I.

Barefoot Summers

Stomping Grounds

inspired by George Ella Lyon's "Where I'm From"

My people sprang from dirt, Scotch-Irish
farmers, Oglethorpe's debtors, bore names
like Royal, Luke, Whitley and Tanner.
Cousins swarmed yards like flies,
picked cotton, put in tobacco,
"Hard work never hurt nobody."

Before chain gangs freed
roadsides of bushes and vines, I foraged
plums and blackberries
along fences that hemmed in swine.

In that place of hand-me-down clothes,
barefoot summers and fishing holes,
I escaped into stories about giant sequoias,
an Inca boy who tended llamas, *A Wrinkle
in Time,* met people who lived in books
Miss Cleo stacked under my arms, sent home
with me from the public library.

Daddy's gas station signed restrooms
MEN, WOMEN, and COLORED. Black maids—
Edna, Annie B, and her mother Beatrice—
ironed church shirts, butchered chickens,
and sang to me of a different future.

"The truth will set you free
when the world is on fire."

US Hwy 129

Tourists travelled the two-lane road
to beaches, gators & orange groves
then headed home after skin
burned or at winter's end when
daffodils yellowed. Many stopped in
our small town for gas, 29¢ a gallon,
mashed potatoes & country steak
at one-cook diners, $1.50, stayed
at mom & pop motels until I-75's higher
speed limits & city bypasses lured drivers
to cookie-cutter chains like Shoney's
& Ho Jo's. A few holdouts drove the
old route, watched towns become outposts,
storefront ghosts.

Snapper Head Bait & Tackle

This shanty once hosted early dawn
anglers, dusk stragglers who bought
red wigglers, chirping crickets, or silver lures
before heading to their favorite ponds.

Women with hair like hornets' nests measured
cane poles against grandchildren's spines. Men
in overalls reached for creek chugs
with triple hooks that ripped gills.

When its owner sold, the new proprietor
parked his RV out back, kept hours
when he felt like it. People quit coming.
That man peddled the shack to a younger man

who, to revive anemic sales, doubled
its goods and girth. The merchandise staled.
That lad added an ice cream display,
checkered tablecloths for customers

in no hurry to fish, offered morning
biscuits and microwaved pizza.
A few regulars dined in the tackle room,
but soon, like the Hardees down the road

that became a Popeyes then closed—
its lighted sign gouged out—this bait shop,
its windows barred, doors locked,
is now no more than local lore.

Elegy for Childhood Trees

The live oak, home to a wooden horse swing,
        showered acorns on pink azaleas. Beside
            the kitchen window, a mimosa bloomed.

My sister picked puffs and pretended to powder her face
        before gliding down a make-believe runway.
            A Bartlett dressed white in spring dropped

yellow globes midsummer—Mama boiled and packed
        pears in Mason jars for a taste of sunshine
            in December—and a Kieffer

my grandmother planted at the old homeplace,
        stooped with ripening fruit, stretched
            its branches like an arthritic hand.

"Plumb crazy," my grandmother would say if she could
        see this poisoning of land, clearcutting of trees,
            for in her day

pecans lined dirt roads, their green-sickle leaves cloaking
        velvet husks that burst to reveal
            tawny shells. If nuts were slow

to fall, we threw sticks, shook limbs.
        In piney woods, gum tapped by descendants
            of slaves yielded turpentine

for sealing ships, dabbing wounds. Cypresses shaded
        swamps and brackish ponds, their knees rising
            from muddy graves, feathery needles harboring

snakes as boats oared by. Magnolias wore sugar blossoms
        the size of dinner plates, blooms Grandmother warned us
            not to touch lest they brown and wilt.

Royal Family Keepsakes

A snuff can and wooden pipe,
bronzed and mounted
on a brass base, rest
on the fireplace mantle.
My mother, the baby of a brood of eight,
who never dipped or smoked,
preserved these relics,
passage back to the steps
where she played after supper
while her parents rocked on the porch,
her mother dipping, father puffing
as they talked church and crops
failing, lame mules and pasty children,
how they would soon
lose the farm.

Snuff

1.

Tobacco cooked and ground
to powder, burnt umber,

sieved soft as White Lily flour,
infused with peach,

strawberry, wintergreen
and funneled into silos

small as half rolls
of silver dollars

then paper strip sealed
and labelled:

Tube Rose
Dixie Sweet
Copenhagen

Mouth cancer.

2.

A tin that fits a girl's palm
        wrapped in a cotton hankie
                tatted with pink pansies

ferried home in a skirt pocket
        from the country store, bait shop
                or gas station,

smuggled to Grandmother
in the nursing home.

3.

A hickory twig, little bigger
than a toothpick,
dipped in grind,
brushed against gums.

Women bent over
wash tubs, weeds,
shelling peas, juice
dripping from lips.

40 minutes
of nicotine bliss.

4.

Some declared snuff a nasty habit,
others an outright sin.

Town ladies dipped
on the sly, hid cans
on kitchen shelves
behind cornmeal and grits,
in lingerie drawers.

5.

At church, old widow Mattie pulled a can from her bosom,
sprinkled the powder into her hand, wet it with spit,
and dabbed the paste on a child's wasp sting.

6.

We girls pretended with a blend—
half-cocoa, half-sugar pinched

into chipmunk cheeks—spat
muddy syrup onto the ground

or into cups we toted
like our aunts and mothers

who warned cigarettes
made a woman look cheap.

Smokehouse Incantation

Hinges whine as I open the forbidden
door, squeeze inside. My head
bumps shoulders and flanks that sag
rafters. The salt so thick, my skin
burns, eyes pool. I crouch closer
to the cool earth, squint in dim light
at dusty shelves crammed with jars
of tomatoes, pickled peaches,
okra spears. My stomach hurts.
Around my bare feet, craters the size
of thumbs pock the ground, homes
for roly polies and ant lions. I hear
my name but dare not respond.
Instead, I pull a broom straw
from my pocket, swivel the tip
in a nearby hole, whisper
"Doodle bug, doodle bug,
your house is on fire; come out,
come out, wherever you are."

Pampas Grass

Sneak out the back door
creep down
        three
            concrete
                steps
run toward silvery plumes that dust
cobwebs from the air.

Turn
sideways,
edge
through
razor-
sharp
leaves
that
veil
a
holy
of holies.

Inside
the cool of darkness
greets. Lie in the dirt
until a high priest appears—
a tri-color collie who forms
a pillow for your head,
licks away your tears.

Forget the threats,
the belt. Pretend
it did not happen.
Sleep.

At dusk, when your mother calls,
peek through the blades. Wait
until she turns her head, then crawl
from under the bushes,
rise and amble across the yard
whistling, as if
you've been playing with friends.

Allegiance

Pooch whined, scratched the front door
each night until a light switched on
and she, granted entry,

circled the poster bed to make
sure we were safe. Once satisfied,
she went outside.

One night she died. The house now mine
I cling like vine, refuse
to patch grooves paws clawed last.

The Lost Art of Making Mud Pies

Play is a child's work.
—Ruth Royal Peterson

Steal into your mother's kitchen.
Open a lower cabinet. Pilfer
a mixing bowl (plastic not glass)
and a measuring cup. Pull a battered
wooden spoon from the utensil drawer.
Place them in a round baking pan
you snitch from that hiding
place beneath the oven.

Cart your stash outside to the faucet
closest to the gardenia bush where
white honeys the air. Sit
on the mulch. Arrange the contraband
around you in a crescent-moon
close enough to work.

Push pine needles aside to expose
soil. Shovel black flour
into your bowl, moisten with water,
and stir, stir, stir. When the mixture
becomes as pliable as dough,
roll it into balls and pat them in the pan,
pressing your small fingers against
the goo until it adheres to the sides.

Set your confection on a picnic table
in the backyard for sun to bake.
Eat lunch. Return with a paper plate
your mother provides, a napkin,
dull knife, and fork. Slice a wedge,
slide onto plate, then sample.

Hopscotch

Dirt and stick
were all a farm child needed.
City kid? Just asphalt and chalk to
scotch a pattern like the one etched in
concrete at the Roman Forum. Nine blocks
stacked atop one another, some resting
side by side, the grid crowned with
a circle labeled London or
Heaven or Home.

Alone or with
friends, you tested
your skills: pitched

rocks sequentially into   blocks, hopped one-legged
without smudging a line,   twirled round and retraced
your path, stopping only   to bend down and retrieve

your stone
a marker for one's
soul in China.

Tight fisted, exiting the   grid, your reward was to
repeat the moves until   your aim failed or you
spilled to the ground. No   referees or written rules

when you
tired, you dragged
your foot

through the clay
or watched as
spring rain

washed
limestone
lines away.

High Steppers

In the fall, when boys
tossed pigskins in sand
lots and spiraled balls
  downfield at
  Friday night
   games, she
   reached for
    white boots
     that hugged
     her calves and
      sported tassels
     which swung
     as she marched
    down the gridiron during halftime
   windmilling flags or twirling a baton,
  sometimes aflame. Strutters. Polished.
    Slick-soled. Gaining ground. Her
     ticket to high
     school fame.

Steady Walkers

A man in a camel suit flattens the girl's feet
on a sliding Brannock Device, asks for her left
heel, then her right. The steel platform

prototyped 25 years earlier with Erector sets
measures a foot four different ways, but it
no longer competes with glowing bones.

When the doctor ordered corrective shoes,
her mother drove a hundred miles to a store
advertising the latest scientific advance—

a Foot-O-Scope that displayed metatarsals
and phalanges, guaranteed accuracy of fit.
No one suspected the box resembling

an upright radio, with viewing stations
at different heights for parents
and children, leaked radioactivity.

The salesman returns to the showroom, lifts
the lid. The girl peers at black and white
Oxfords with built-up arches. Little room

for toes to wiggle, sure
to stand out on a playground
of red and blue Keds, but stepping

in and out of the fluoroscope
leaves no doubt. She must wear them
whatever the cost.

TV Trilogy

for Brownie

Four horsemen corral
teenage fans who pine for a
Ponderosa life.

Nose twitches. Bewitched
dishes levitate from sink.
Lone broom sweeps kitchen.

"Beam me up, Scotty,"
Brownie prays, tells the nurse,
"No more dialysis."

When I Believed

Sprawled
       on dappled ground   I gaze
                  through crowns.

      Jets   cross   midair;
        my curls wave.

      Can people up there glimpse gold?

At night
       riding the double Ferris wheel

      I finger heaven's edge,   stretch
        for Orion's star-studded belt.

      Do babies hear angels swishing?

That was when I believed
       Earth a stopover   and people

        could fly away home.

November 22, 1963

I was riding in the back seat
of my parents' blue Buick

headed to Ocilla's Sweet Potato
Festival when the radio blared

"President Kennedy's been shot!"
and I wondered if people who'd voted

against him because he was Catholic
or too rich or too young felt bad

or secretly glad as people might
if a president they despised was downed

by a gun, and while the news spread,
my friends and I sat in the school

auditorium, its wooden seats
bolted to the floor,

paused with others to pray for our country
then cheered for beauty

contestants whose solos and taps
echoed off walls.

Bobwhites

The landowner flushed a covey of quail
as he strode down a row of dead pines,
the birds a sign all would be well.

A hunter built a blind. After bagging a whitetail
he climbed down, marched across jessamine vines
where his boots flushed a covey of quail.

While burning a longleaf stand, a forester in overalls
photographed firebirds taking flight, a divine
reminder, the quail, that all would be well.

Before naval stores and peckerwood mills
children hunted for nests along fence lines,
their footsteps flushing coveys of quail

across dirt roads into cotton fields,
chicks and parents in single file, their aligned
presence a sign all would be well.

If a lover of forests today parts the veil
at day's dusk or morning's dawn
and hears *poor bob white* whistled by quail,
she may pause and pray that all will be well.

Initiation at Jekyll Island

It happened the summer I turned
ten at the Golden Isle's historic inn,
once a millionaires' playground, not home
where I could hide, no ocean or pool
in sight, but on my family's one-week vacation

that I noticed a pale spot then a full flow,
the one I read about in a pamphlet
my mother shoved into my hands
a few months earlier saying,
"If you have questions, we'll talk later."

Me? Questions? Not after illustrations
depicting body parts with anatomic
names and diagrams of how
they fit together, followed by:
"Don't get pregnant."

Trapped at the beach, I could wear
my new two-piece and laze in the sun
but never tell boys eager to toss me
in the water that I was indisposed.
A clued-in father stepped to my chaise,

pressed quarters into my palms. Alone,
I retreated to the arcade where games
with flashing names hunkered walls,
fed coins to the gods, flippered silver
balls at targets that clacked and dinged.

"Later" came the week of my wedding,
bearing its own bells and whistles.
Mama stuck her head into my room,
cleared her throat, and said
"About that talk—"

Taking My Leave

inspired by Bruce Smith's "Goodbye Tuscaloosa"

Farewell to Myrtle and Myrtice, Vasthi and Saphroni,
Rubye Herow and Special Edna, whose DNA I share;
to Frank Ladies Circle, farm wives who pray
    and the First Monday Bridge Club, card gossipers.

Goodbye to the Royal Sing, where snow cones cooled
children boiling in the sun and quartets ate
    Brunswick stew made from
    hogs' heads (little did they know).

No more *too big for your britches,*
bless your heart, keep quiet.

So long Mabel Brown's history class, so boring we gazed
outside at grazing cows and *sayonara* Flannery O'Connor.
Peacocks did not blind you with their beauty
    and, yes, a good man *is* hard to find.

Adios to Uncle Roger's pond, Mama squealing when she reeled in
a bass, and to Uncle Buck's *Phantom of the Opera* face
    carved by blades from a corn combine when his shirt
    tangled. Thanks to the sharecropper who saved him

while black bodies sank to muddy creek bottoms
and thanks to the silenced women
who floated Christmas camellias in candy dishes
    filled with clear water.

No more hiding in closets from
twisters, belts, shotguns.

I'm leaving behind Jefferson Davis State Park, where Union
soldiers captured Dixie's leader fleeing in his wife's overcoat,
    and the dirt road, where surrounded by a cricket chorus
    I first made out, warnings about bad girls pushed

far from sight, and gardens where I gathered legacies
of enslaved Africans—black-eyed peas that could not see
and okra cut in pre-dawn light to lessen its sting. I was your
    fair-haired child until I opened my eyes.

Now you no longer
see me.

II.

The Waking

Home Movies

Christmas plays, homecoming
parades, dogs rolling in dirt,
teenagers twisting
to Chubby Checker.

My sister and I peer
as faces flicker past,
pull memories like popcorn
from a shared bag.

What's her name?
Count the candles quick.

That's the Tuckers' house.
Five. No, six.

Infants age
into snaggle-toothed youths,
women wear hats,
men chat at a gas station,
then spy the camera
and walk toward the brown box
with wind-up key
as if to crawl inside
to see . . .
to see what?

We don't remember
Mama flashing her smile
or Daddy jumping the waves
but they do in these movies.

By the time we had eyes
the Bell & Howell film
had been traded for Kodak slides,
perfect for photos of funeral flowers.

Embrace

The trip from recliner to table
too much for my mother,
she now rides to breakfast
on wheels that bump
furniture, scrape doorjambs.

I am learning this contraption,
its accordion ways, how to fold
and unfold the seat,
set the brakes, turn and lift
my mother's dead weight
into its waiting arms.

The tombstone is paid for, eulogy
written. Funeral plans dictate
how to lay her to rest: blue nightgown,
closed casket, white lilies.

For years, Daddy wanted to engrave
their marker so *she* could view it,
or so he said.
Mama protested, but today, rolling
back to hospital bed, turns her chin,
says, *Tell him to go ahead.*

par•tic•u•lar•i•ty

par•tic•u•lar•i•ty n. 1a. *a minute detail:* like the mole on your back, the one you worry will grow or blacken, the one you keep asking the doctor to check. b. *individual characteristic; singularity:* as in a face on the planet mirrored by no one else, your face dressed with a beauty pageant smile as singular as your thumbprint, eyeball, or vocal vibration. 2. *the quality of being particular, distinguished from universal:* such as the name given you at birth, so you are not any girl or daughter, but one-of-a-kind, and even when you meet others christened the same or read about a character in a children's book who shares your name, the way you sign that name distinguishes you. 3a. *attentiveness to detail:* the way you comb your hair to the side or tithe to the church, ten percent to the penny, or how a single corpuscle shoots the rapids in your clogged veins. b. *the state of being fastidious in behavior or expression:* as when you measure the tequila, two ounces and not a drop more, for your evening margarita, the drink you drag a walker to the kitchen to mix, even though dragging is not fastidious. 4. *in Christian theology:* as in Jesus, the One, Spirit and Flesh, who lived, died, and will come again, and as much as other religions are gaining ground, your wager is on a Savior beyond comprehension to a binary mind, a particularity, as real and juicy and sweet as Eve biting into an apple, damning the whole story into existence.

Cleaning Out My Mother's Closet

Polyester plaids,
        stone-washed jeans,
                and a navy wool coat
will soon hang

in give-away closets
        dank with mold,
                on hall trees

at sidewalk sales,

from racks at thrift-stores
        —LuLu's, the BeeHive,
                Second Time Around—

await new owners.   If none come,

volunteers will bundle the clothes
        and ship them abroad
                or rip them into rags.

Is their recycled fate better than

pin-striped suits
        split down the back
                to accommodate corpses,
silk nightgowns
        shrouded over shells
                of departed souls—

garments destined to survive

casketed bodies
      facing east
            awaiting resurrection?

A Triptych on the First Anniversary of My Mother's Death

in memory of Dorothy Eloise Royal Luke

1

What's heaven like? Mama asked three weeks
before she died. She was sitting
on a red couch, frail, her eyes closed.
Light through the picture window
streaked her white hair gold.

I recalled tales of paved streets and pearly gates,
said, *I don't know, but it must be . . .
wonderful, full of love.*

Earth's pretty wonderful too, she replied.

2

Mama had come from the womb of a cripple—
a miracle, declared spinster aunts who asked
for the child if it lived, but predicted the death of both.

How my grandmother, felled by a stroke when her belly
was ripe, gave birth and then lived thirty years
to see me born is a mystery. Rocking on the front porch

to ease her pain, Grandma would fret over her yard,
then rise, hobble down the steps, dragging
a straw broom behind, and with one hand

sweep the South Georgia sand, tracing patterns
that rose in her head, like lines drawn by Navajo
medicine men and Zen masters she never knew.

Satisfied, winded from her work, she would limp
back up the stairs, collapse into her chair
and dare anyone to desecrate the designs.

Mama would bake cakes when she was upset,
swirling divinity icing into patterns
reminiscent of her mother's swept sand yard.

The night she died, kin and caregivers
surrounded her bed, recited the twenty-third
psalm to bid her farewell.

We dressed her corpse in a blue nightgown,
sang gospel songs, lowered
the coffin into the ground.

3

Sun strikes the bench where I sit staring
at winter grass that carpets her grave,
dates etched in marble's blue veins.
A sandpiper prances nearby.

Love blankets me, just as it covered Mama
the night she left her body for us to bury, just as
it warmed my grandmother when she edged
toward death . . . then returned to bear life.

Nourishment

Once biscuits airy as clouds dripped
butter, floated in chicken
gravy, or swam in liquid gold—
syrup boiled from juice extracted
by a mule hitched to a pole, an owner
prodding it to hoove in stubborn circles,
grind cane stalks. Bread from maize
filled our bellies; hush puppies
spooned from grease were
tossed to hunting dogs and whining
children while fish fried.
Now I nibble on flapjacks
made of flour from roots and nuts
and hunger for a taste of childhood.

Kitchen Lament

i.

Brandished as a weapon when no rolling pin's
in sight. Home to Grandma's crackling
cornbread. Hot seat for battered chicken,
okra, green tomatoes—everything Southern fried.
Never darkened the inside of a dishwasher;
instead, hand scoured, oiled then stored
on stove's eye. Cast iron ready
for the next round of sear and sizzle.

ii.

Displayed on yellow Formica, a place of honor
in Mama's kitchen. Sunbeam's glass bowl
slid from center to side as beaters whisked yolks
warm from the hen house into creamed sugar and butter.
Spoonfuls of White Lily followed, then milk drizzled
over swirling batter, a lemon pound cake in the making.
Years later, the mixer languished in a bottom cabinet,
replaced by a blender that churned out peach smoothies.

iii.

Defrost, heat, warm, reheat. Third time round for this
cup of java. Inside, eggs splatter, bagels rubberize.
Instant oatmeal's a better choice for a time saver
that renders food tasteless in minutes. Granted,
there's no mess. Cooking's quick. Nuke a single serving
of Stouffer's lasagna or Lean Cuisine's rice and beans,
stand at the sink to eat. Toss plastic in the bin
(black, can't recycle) then head back to the screens.

Break of Day

I sit on blacktop in my nightgown—
to dress would miss the light.

An orange sun fans
the horizon, warms

a field of cotton, bolls scarcely open.
Cows moo, sounding a call

to matins. Rusted iron posts
strung with empty lines await

clothes that will not be hung.
The fig tree, backlit bare,

a stark reminder
of my mother's death.

My father needs help with tasks
he once taught me—balancing

a checkbook, saying his prayers.
The grudges, spankings, family fights

fade with last night's bad dreams,
swept away with the waking.

Hooked

After her death,
he glued brass
plaques onto
items he feared
family might
sell or haul to
landfill: the
black piano
where his
quartet had
practiced,
the desk
where she'd
squinted.
A table from
Joe's Pool Hall.   A pie
safe labeled—   *This is not a*
family heirloom.   *We bought it be-*
 cause we liked it.   Memories snipped
   from faded   days
   hooking   offspring
    just as she'd   snagged an
       8 pound, 4 ounce wide-mouth bass at her
         sister's pond in 1961, the fish they'd
          taxidermied, the one now hanging
               in a grandson's home.

Prodigal

The father who watched and waited to greet
a penitent child with robe, ring and feast

now in his grave, no longer grieves
the excuses you made, the lies he believed.

If one day you wake, walk down the road
and pause at his grave, you'll carry the load

of knowing he asked before he died
that you come home, sit by his side.

Visit you did, but the years had flown
with living too hard, all innocence gone.

He needed a boy to put things straight,
did not recognize your bearded face.

So you leaned in, fingered a badge
pinned to your shirt, hoping to snatch

his memory back. Etched there in red,
the name you shared.

Prayer for a Dying Father

Take my father now, Lord. Not next month
or next week. Not even tomorrow.
Don't wait for the grans' Thanksgiving visit.
Don't let him live another Christmas.
He's ninety-one, has seen the wayward son
he wanted to lay eyes on one more time,
and that promise his baby sister made
to come—three years he held out hope.
Now she's too sick to travel,
said her goodbye over the phone.
So why wait?
Take him before he drools,
wears Depends, before bed sores
eat his flesh. Take him while
he still tucks a handkerchief
into the pocket of his red silk pajamas,
motions me closer, whispers
I have been so blessed.

III.

Gravity

Midway

He relished
the roller coaster
its glacial clicking
swooping dive

couldn't abide
the Ferris Wheel
her favorite ride.
At night,
seat stopped
on top, lights
dazzled the girl
he loved.

After *I do's*
they compromised:

zigzagged
in the Scrambler
like bees swarming a hive

mounted horses
that poled
up
and down
metronome
hooves
pounding time

stumbled
through the Fun House
she pointing out his Pinocchio nose
he her Fat Lady belly
lost one another

for a time
navigated that maze alone

belted themselves
into Bumper Cars
sideswiped
then rammed
each other

landed in a Tilt-a-Whirl
swinging
side to side
until a full swirl
fused their bodies
like the night
they first danced
like bugs caught
in cotton candy.

True Believers

The parents dreamed of a Disney trip
with their children. Each generation
had to visit the castle, meet the mouse.
When time came for the grand

adventure, youngsters stood on tip
toes to buy a storybook vacation.
Inside the gates, they found a madhouse:
Mickey posing with fans on the main strand,

babies balanced on mothers' hips
as ice cream dripped. First aid stations
filled with temporary orphans. Quarreling spouses
tolerating tag-along grandmothers who fanned

faces with wet handkerchiefs and iron-gripped
the hands of toddlers begging to pet Dalmatians,
fly with Dumbo, or duck into the house
of the seven Dwarfs. Yet, this family remained

true believers, joined snaking lines, whistled *Zip-
a-Dee-Doo-Dah,* rode Thunder Mountain,
got off thoroughly doused
and eager to go again.

gra•vi•ty

gra•vi•ty *n.* 1a. *dignity or sobriety,* as in giving a eulogy and laying a father to rest, or the sobriety an alcoholic seeks when joining AA; b. *seriousness of situations,* like wedding vows followed by a spouse's affair or the word cancer catching in a sister's throat. 2. *a weight or heaviness* that a woman feels with a gun to her head or in a lockdown ward after shock treatment. 3a. *the attraction of Earth for bodies near the surface,* like the pull a birthplace has on a girl and if she defies gravity, floats free, will she drift weightless through life or splash down at another site where water and the moon's pull will rock her to sleep?

Twelve Letters

lined up like soldiers
dare her to decide.
Shred? Re-read then shred?
Save for yet another decade?

She'd promoted the dispatches
from a filing drawer to a place of honor, out
in the open on her writing desk. Here they're at rest
awaiting dismissal: four plain envelopes

and eight air mailers, the latter flagged
red and blue. Missives penned
after her college debating partner
had won the lottery,

a single digit draft number
that guaranteed him a tour in Vietnam.

She hadn't read them since '71,
when the last post arrived, her maiden
name inked out, in its place *Mrs.*
She'd stashed that letter in a drawer

with the others, prayed there'd be another.
The cache survived a divorce, seven moves
and repeated purgings. Now fingering
an envelope's fold, she recalls the night

Justin made his decision. After a practice round,
he confided he was dropping out, enlisting.
No use waiting, he said.
Probably won't make it back anyway.

All she could muster:
Please write.

Ghosts

in memory of Zim

Shudder to think of the load
this big-ass Mama's hauling, boxes
painted with skulls and crossbones.
St. Chris swings from the rear-view
mirror, guaranteeing protection
or entrance to paradise.
I'm not Catholic,
but I'm sure saints kept me alive
in Nam, so I'm casting
my lot with him.

I skate over a bridge, blinkers
flashing, then my 18-wheels grind
up a mountain road whose curves
refuse to bend. Run-away ramps—
little more than apparitions—hide
beneath snow sheets. Wish I had
no mortgage or mouths to feed.

After my tour, I tried to settle down
on the family farm. Harrowing rows
dawn to dusk didn't silence the screams
in my head. Nightmares haunted
no matter how many pills I gulped.
To live, I had to run. Bought a Mack.
Told Mary Ann, "When the kids grow up,
you can ride shotgun." But for now,
it's just me and the ghosts
moaning over the engine's rumble.
Sometimes I drive 36 hours
on no more fuel than a catnap

and a gallon of coffee.
In Nam, I once went a week
without sleep, no coffee needed.

Better to keep rolling, beat the deadline.
I listen to music I once spun at high school
proms, tunes I disc-jockeyed
in war zones littered with trees
and bodies charred by napalm.

Hey Jude
I Can't Get No Satisfaction
Born to Be Wild—

that's me, wild, wilder than
when I dodged linebackers,
scored touchdowns, believed
speed would save me from the draft,
wilder than when I drag raced
my souped-up Chevy. Not much different
playing chicken with big rigs.

I've careened up and down
these mountains for ten years now,
topped 100 on stretches
through cornfields, prairies and deserts
goading God. Seems like death breathing
down my neck's the only thing brings
me alive. I gun the gas, urge the truck
to skid, imagine exploding
like my buddies when they tripped
on a land mine or held a grenade too long.

Tomorrow,
when the sun rises,
I'll crest the Rockies.
Never saw those peaks
until I took to the road.
Now I can say one thing
for sure: This country
is as beautiful
as the song claims—
from sea to shining sea.

Choose Life

. . . so that you and your children may live.
Deuteronomy 30:19b

A raging teen storms two flights of stairs,
appears in the bedroom doorway, flings

words like ice from a pail:
You're a bitter old woman!

This pimple-faced son who knows
nothing of infidelity dares to declare

Get on with your life
or I'll go stark, raving mad.

That night she vows there'll be laughter
in the house before he's fledged.

Two years later, in the kitchen
after a baseball win, they joke, chug Cokes.

He dwarfs his sunburned fan.
She eyes his dirt-caked uniform,

rakish grin, reminds him
of the evening he named her sin.

Bitter, he sputters. *No way!*
Crazy maybe.

Heading for Home

for Jonathan

Bases loaded, one run down
full count, two outs.
A high school senior
steps into the batter's box
taps home plate
hoists bat, focuses on the pitcher
awaiting the catcher's signal,
a state playoff in the balance.

His grandfather, eyes closed,
lies dying in a hospital bed,
a radio beside him blaring.
Recruited after high school
by the Saint Louis Cardinals,
he and the boy share a given name
and a build that favors them
in the sport: big thighs,
tight strike zone,
strong wrists.

No matter how
the young man swings,
or if he gets caught looking,
they both know this moment
will tag him for the rest
of his life weighted with memories
of his grandfather's advice
during Little League games
and after tournaments played
with the same guys
now stubble-jawed teens

who hang in the dugout chomping
sunflower seeds or juicing
tobacco onto red clay,
their caps clutched, afraid
to watch, afraid not.

Radio announcer delivers
the play:
pitcher's shake off
nod to the catcher
slow windup
sinker to the plate.
Batter swings—
wood cracks

white ball wings toward the lights
        as grandfather listens
        going
                going

Metamorphoses

for Jackson

Once a kid with a buzz cut
who trapped tree frogs

and admired their glisten,
then a teen with sexy

spikes who borrowed his mom's
gel. Now he tames his blond

hair, grown long for head
shots, in a ponytail.

For the camera, he loosens
his locks, brushes

them across his brow to
highlight marble blue eyes,

combs tresses behind one
ear then grimaces and grins

to portray an addict, a pusher,
a European prince or

a rock star making love
to his Fender guitar.

Gray Matter

Forgetting is what I do these days—
    names of relatives, deceased pets,
        which apples pucker my lips,
            the password for my credit cards.

Crowded by birthdays and funerals,
    synapses no longer fire or remember
        to turn off the stove's eye.

Once, I could recite Bible verses,
    rattle off the periodic table.
        Now words retreat when I reach
            for that shepherd psalm.

Notes on bathroom mirror, car
    dashboard remind *buy skim milk,*
        pick up grandchild, hair cut at 9.

Aging in Place

Has the time come?
Will I know?
Who will show me?

Will I be
out of place or
all over the place?

What happened to *Oh,
the Places You'll Go?*
Must I give up

my grandmother's chair?
Is staying put a placebo?
How much will it cost

my heirs?
Where else would I go?
Does one have to know

one's place
to age with grace?
Will anyone visit me there?

IV.

Coming Down through the Women's Line

Learning to Float

Raking books
    from bulging shelves,
        I bid farewell

    to college companions,
        J. Krishnamurti & W. J. Cash;

    good riddance to self-help
        Beattie, Peck, & Covey's seven.

You have served me well—
    but I'm breaking

        like I did that day at the ocean

    when I asked my mother
        to remove her hands
            from my back,
        closed my eyes
                trusted
        the swells
             the rise
          the fall
            of moon-spun waves
            lapping my face.

Night View from a Bedroom Window

She hides her shine behind the clouds, flirts with stars
I cannot see, winks at planets and galaxies I trust
are there even though the dark obscures
such love affairs; and stories of a face
in her crescent shape or werewolves
howling when she is full
tease in a universe of quarks and strings
where jazz cats belt her pull
the same pull that guides
tides, morphs flat-chested girls
into full-breasted women
mothers and daughters
who fear the silver
disc may one night
follow her shadow
into the sea
forsake
her cycles
forget
to lure
moonflowers
into
midnight
bloom.

Application

She X's
the block
that marks her
from birth,
the one
that also marks
her daughter

a majority
lured
by promises
of cracked
ceilings
while wages
wilt children
whimper
at home
on the stove
supper burns.

Glenmary Sister

for Maureen

Fresh out of high school, a novice in a shortened habit
scoured remote hollers, visited coal camps, argued scrip

was little more than slave wages if miners could only spend it
at the company store, accompanied a teenage mother

to DC to testify about hunger. One night, on call in those coves,
she rounded a curve as rocks avalanched onto the road.

Boulders would have crushed her
had she not braked, swerved.

Fifty years later, no longer a nun, this grandmother
points out roadside tipples, some abandoned, others groaning.

She protests machines ripping open seams
in a field named Pocahontas. Ridges, more mesa

than mountain top, loom as locomotives
heaped with Wise County coal—blasted chunks

of ancient sunshine—snake through a tunneled gorge;
their load, scabs of black gold, to warm fine new homes.

Women on the Ohoopee

Our guide hefts kayaks
                from a black Ford pickup
        as easily as a man

        slips the one-seaters
                into tea-colored water
                        knee-deep.

    We climb in
                dip our paddles
                        glide.

        Along the bank   red fruit dangles
    from tupelos   like bauble earrings.

        Downriver   we beach our boats
                on a whim   strip
                    for a season's last swim.

Sisters: Take Two

If that late-night call
      had been a scene in a movie,

I'd have asked the director
      for a reshoot

from the moment I let you dangle
      on the phone, so weary

was I of listening. You tried to tell me
      you were tired of living,

checking off last things to do.
      I refused such news,

insisted you were fine—
      lymphoma in remission,

had to be depression talking—
      and began a litany of your blessings

naming them one by one
      like the old hymn taught us:

good husband, roof over your head,
      food on the table,

and all the while my lips puckered
      like they did when as kids

we sucked sour juice from grapes
    along Aunt Ruth's fence,

my voice sharp
    as her butcher knife.

On Blue Days

I return in my mind to a mother,
two daughters rushing surf,

"Last one in is a rotten egg."
The orange musk

of Coppertone on bodies
past their prime, our noses flush

with brine. A mercury dime
washed ashore years ago,

your sign to buy the haven
where we later feasted

on sweet scallops and
each other's lives. Flapping

blue shade, painted red toes,
jellyfish stinging thighs,

the lifeguard's whistled warning
winged too quickly by.

Runes

for Kerri

A butterfly inked
across shoulder blade
as she left for college.
Her second, Mickey Mouse
grinning from a buttock
to mark the birth
of a boy. Twin flames
on a breast when she wed,
a ribbon at the ankle
when blessed with a daughter.
Pyramids in her thirties
needled from inner wrist
to elbow. More skin at forty:
spirit animal sleeves, wolf
and bear cascading
down outer arms
beside pine cones
and mountain peaks,
to ground.

Remnants

A pile of *Life, Look,* and *National Geographic*
three feet high lean against the walnut chest

that housed her jeans before she left for college.
She now reaches across the heap, opens the top

drawer to Butterick patterns and fabric folded
in squares. Red gingham for a tablecloth

her mother will never stitch, a floral print
her daughter will never sashay,

and three yards of lavender linen—
an Easter outfit with pearl buttons

waiting for the Singer to be cleared
of wrapping paper and Christmas cards.

Buttons

i.

In a Mason jar on a shelf
above Aunt Ruth's Singer,
the collection more valued than coins.

Circles, squares, half-moons, roses. Stark white
and Crayola shades prismed with light.

The first: a seashell from the Indus Valley, 5000 BC.
Then bone, horn, ivory, wood, pottery, flint.
Gold, silver, copper. Diamonds, rubies, marble, glass.
Plastic.

Pea-sized pearls
hard to unfasten
string the backs
of wedding gowns.

ii.

Needle threads in and out of eyes.
A seamstress ties a double knot,
clenches teeth, bites.

Without buttonholes,
nothing more than decoration.

Chipped button? A mother
searches for a twin or look-alike
from a stash of orphans.

Shirt buttons on the right for men;
easier to reach for weapons. Why
on the left for women?

How does one button one's lips?

In medieval times a button plucked
from one's jacket covered one's debts.

Did buttons dream
of a future as mini-phones,
listening devices,
data collectors?

Hooks and eyes,
Velcro and straight pins
aspire to buttons' work
but lack a flair for fashion.

A loose button hangs its head.

Homage to the Least

for Diane

~ 1 ~

O tubular wonder, incomparable tunnel digger,
master soil builder coveted by gardeners
and anglers alike, creature

without eyes, nose, or ears whose muscular mass
contracts and releases in waves, moves
through dirt and hard packed clay,

you go by many names ~ night crawler, red wiggler
angleworm ~ an alchemist who composts rotten
scraps, fungi, even cardboard

into sweet-smelling castings. You convert
garbage into loam like Jesus turned
water into wine. In turn,

others consume you ~ robins, moles, foxes, bears.
Each spring we plant and weed
flower beds, pray to find

your kind among roots of columbine and daffodils,
each autumn under leaf debris, chomping away.
We walk in parks, through fields

and forests, with little thought of you under foot.
Rain washes you from your home.
Stranded in the sun

on asphalt and concrete, your body
dries like a leather shoestring
or worn rubber band.

~ 2 ~

Turning over a clod, the yard man
       spies two tubes, red-gray,
wriggling in the clay: an earthworm severed
       by the garden shovel
in his hands. Unlike the primitive
       planarian and
despite what he's been told, the writhing tail
       will never grow
a second head, and although the mouth might sprout
       a tail, this unearthed
night crawler will never become bait,
       squirm like its kin
looped on hooks then cast into ponds
       where wiggles and waves
lure bluegills and largemouth bass
       toward evening meals.

~ 3 ~

Digging a hole
with my four-year-old
grandson, tow-headed
and sun-freckled, I watch
       him encounter you for the first time.
       As you curl and coil in his palm, he turns
       and asks, "Can I keep him?"
I explain a worm will die
if removed from the soil.
He carefully places
you back in your home.

We plant a dwarf red maple seedling above you,
just as I hope my grandson will plant an oak
or dogwood above the hole where I'm buried
shroud-cloaked,
three feet under, not six,
so you can tunnel
through my remains.

~ 4 ~

The night you presented yourself,
inching toward the surface
to mate, what lesson did you come to teach?

Even though a hermaphrodite, you still needed
another with five beating hearts
to reproduce, affirm life.

~ 5 ~

Years before a grandson was born, I dreamed
of earthworms, hordes of them, teeming masses
in every clump of mud
I dug. I was in a contest to see how many
I could find. Others discovered
one or two, but the worms showed themselves to me ~
writhing balls like snakes teeming from Medusa's head.
Embarrassed by my abundance, I stashed them
in a gallon jar, poked holes in the lid then hid
them behind my back. There they began
to glow so bright that I had to bury
them once again
to save our secret.

Deconstructing Goldilocks

Ugly old woman or girl with fair
hair? Lost in the woods or lured
into the forest? Whichever

version of the tale you choose,
the chair breaks, the broth spills,
and the bed is filled with a babe

who does not belong
there, in that room,
with those bears,

and no matter how many homes
one peers into, none are *just right,*
and many a mother

has told a daughter, it doesn't matter
if your bed is too soft or too hard,
"If you make it, you have to lie in it."

And lie in it Goldilocks did,
through two centuries
as bards altered her from

hag into naughty child with silver
then golden hair, and then into a lass
eating porridge, plumping pillows

because too many stories featured
nasty old crones, and the once
frightful tale of a mother

rescuing her daughter from grizzlies
became a damsel longing for hearth,
dating one man too hot, another too cold,

a third just right until she wakes in his bed,
jumps from the story, and exits through
a window that has always been open.

V.

What We Do to Earth

South Georgia Pilgrimage

i.

Past watch towers, barbed wire, and concrete
       cells housing 1500 men

(here, years ago, my father
       visited a man who killed a friend)

past a potter's field, small white crosses
       marking unknown felons' graves,

down a washboard road
       to an 1850s farmhouse,

       white two-story trimmed in green,
          front steps leading

to a wrap-around porch flanked with rockers.
       Out back, sheets flap.

ii.

Not the usual site for a sacred journey,
no hordes to bump shoulders like those
in Jerusalem, Assisi, or Dharamshala.

just me and a few other women searching for peace
and healing at Red Earth Farm where Janisse
and Raven grow heirlooms, Brandywines

and Candy Roasters, herd goats and swap
eggs for a neighbor's caramel cake. Here on retreat,
we feast on biscuits and butterbeans, drink milk

thick with cream from Jerseys grazing by the back
door. Fields once fleeced with cotton teem
with persimmons, may haws, and plums.

iii.

We roam graveyards, visit
remnants of old growth forests
where mother trees share
Mary's grief, bow
at the entrance of burrows,
catacombs for gopher turtles.
A song in a field leads
to the nest of a Bachman's sparrow.
Ohoopee's water flows
like blood in Earth's veins.

iv.

Beside a campfire, spirits
of ancestors hover—
Jim, Ella, Oscar, Odessa,
and ones I do not know—

folks may not believe it so
this brush against my shoulder,
whole body shiver,
whispering in my ear

Speak our names aloud.
We were once here.

v.

No, it is not fireflies or a breeze
or my imagination there as flames sputter
and faces swirl with messages,
not saints or miracle workers
but crackers and convicts for whom
Wiregrass Georgia was holy land,
the place they birthed and buried,
a flock of kin I fled
and to whom I have returned.

I remove a burnt marshmallow from
a stick, open my lips,
and receive the confection
like consecrated bread.

The Seedlings Speak

We, the longleaf pines you plant,
will redeem the land your ancestors
tilled to feed the world.

Tortoises will burrow beneath roots
plunged deep to withstand drought; quail
nest in needled ground. Our branches

will shade eight-point bucks, and,
in time, even your descendants
will be welcome.

Monoculture

"He wanted a forest, not timber."
—Robin Wall Kimmerer

He dreamed of a forest on ancestral land
not pines lined shoulder to shoulder in cornstalk
rows prescribed in the conservation plan.

Green seedlings left to grow at will,
fan former fields, never become junk
mail or paperbacks. He dreamed of tortoises,

sixty years digging homes for skunks,
foxes and snakes, not management
for maximum yield but a world

of wiregrass and sacred groves.
Heirs planned, when their time came,
to mow the longleafs down, haul his dream

of a forest to a mill, rather than lose
the land to taxes and bills.

Flashback at Pearson's Chapel

I've not played a church piano in forty years
and hunger to stride down the aisle,

sit at the black bench, uncover the upright's keys
and strike up a tune that lives in muscle memory—

Ties That Bind or *What a Friend.*
Preacher drones while in my mind

I finger *do, re, mi's* that hieroglyph pages
in Stamps-Baxter songbooks and *Pilgrim's Hymnals,*

the notes' pull as strong as sunrays. Few
winced at sour notes or missed beats so glad

for children like me who clung to the old rugged cross
and plunged beneath a blood-filled fountain, a world

where hymns were badges of belonging—
O For a Thousand Tongues and *Love Lifted Me.*

I traveled far from these walls, learned
to applaud virtuosos who accompanied

chancel choirs, to admire Gregorian chants, even
sing lyrics flashing across sanctuary screens until

I no longer recalled the scales and chords
Miss Ora taught me. Time and decorum may ordain

I remain a prisoner in this pew, but how long?
Nostalgia be damned. How long?

To Keep from Speaking

History is not what is past but what is present.
—James Baldwin

"I am not *your* Negro,"
declares the lone person of color
dining at a table with friends.
We've just watched the James Baldwin
documentary: scenes in which John Wayne
guns down savages, sunlight blondes
Doris Day's hair while
      unnamed dark-skinned men
            hang from trees,

and white faces jeer
as police escort
Dorothy Counts, a spindly girl,
into a Charlotte high school
      spittle dripping
      from her hem.

After ordering wine, a young couple
speak of their four children,
      two Anglo, one Haitian,
         the youngest biracial,
of how they carefully prepare
before going to the park,
church, or grocery store:
      no loud behavior,
      mismatched clothing,
      rumpled hair
to fuel gossip, stares. "Makes me so mad
I can't see straight," the mother says.

A nun who nursed patients
in Thailand then Rwanda, reaches
for bread, confesses her failure
  to fathom the rage that filled
    the screen, stalks the streets.

I sip tea
to keep from speaking
  about James Irwin's lynching
near my home town

and even though it happened
two decades before I was born,
  I still hear
    the baying of hounds.

Perch on a Bank

Scales glisten and gills flare
as fish unhooked and tossed
to the side flip-flop
in knee-high grass
inches from creekflow,
frantic,
until time stills
and death ripens
the air.

A Sign

Tornadoes roar
through mountain valleys
    old-timers once swore
          safe
  from high winds and hurricanes.

Ridges calmed their fury, slowed
  their spin
        before hotter days
  welcomed twisters
   like the one that
      javelined
 swing sets
     twirled
    SUVs and hoisted
     a warehouse
   as if a matchbox
 only to
  drop it
   ten blocks away.
     That funnel vanished
    as quickly as it formed
    retracting its
   locomotive howls
  into clouds
 from which
it spawned.

Warriors for Life

inspired by the documentary For the Next 7 Generations

I will not write a pretty poem
filled with glitzy words while
glaciers melt, rivers reek, and children
starve behind barbed wire, while
loss of bellied, hooved, and winged
precedes our own extinction, while
my kin scuttle ancient teachings,
fashion gadgets into golden calves.

From where will our help come?

from women, who oracles foretold
would lead in the last days,
grandmothers of thirteen moons
and thirteen planets who gathered
from the four directions
to shake the world awake

from African rainforests
        the Alaskan tundra
the mountains of Oaxaca
        Nepal and Tibet
from the Amazon and Columbia rivers
        from Dakota's Black Hills
from Nicaragua

shamans, herbalists, *curanderos,* mediums,
        medicine women, and spiritual leaders
coming together to circle the globe
        visit each other's villages
share healing wisdom.

Let us call their names:

Agnes Baker Pilgrim   Rita Pitka Blumenstein
Aama Bombo   Julieta Casimiro   Flordemayo
Clara Shinobu Iura   Bernadette Rebienot
sisters Rita and Beatrice Long Visitor Holy Dance
Mona Polacca   Tsering Dolma Gyaltong
Maria Alice Campos Freire   Margaret Behan

In Dharamshala, blessed by the Dalai Lama.

In Rome, denied an audience.

And there are others—Alice Walker,
Carol Moseley Braun, Gloria Steinem,
bell hooks, Tenzin Palmo, Joy Harjo,
Robin Wall Kimmerer, Jane Goodall,
Wilma Mankiller
                              and you
if you dare
because thirteen are not enough
to span chasms of hate and genocide

            thirteen hundred are not enough
            to bear Earth's groans

                  thirteen thousand—a start

                        thirteen million a rising tide

                        what we do to Earth
                        we do to us.

Living Room

Windows flank the cottage,
frame pasture outside. Some

days panes prism light so
bright it hurts eyes to gaze

at goats grazing nearby;
other days, mist clouds glass,

blurs the fire inside. The
view depends upon where

I stand, the view ever
changing from where I am.

Summoned

Crouched on a panther
—legs straddling feline's back
arms looped around his neck—
woman rides as the cat muscles
up a chill mountain trail
through dense oaks
red and white
     a bouquet
of daisies and roses clutched
to her breast, an offering
     to whatever guides
or gods called her to this journey
should she encounter them
in this realm where
travel and time
twine with the smell of smoke
her only hint of a campfire
where she might warm herself
     or a cabin
where Grand
     and Great Grand
          and Great-Great Grandmothers
stand behind a door
     stacked like books
          wisdom without end.

About the Author

Karen Luke Jackson draws upon oral history, contemplative practices, and the natural world for inspiration. Her poems and stories have appeared in numerous journals including *Ruminate, Broad River Review, One, Friends Journal, Channel Magazine, Emrys Journal,* and *Leaping Clear.* Karen's debut poetry chapbook *GRIT* (Finishing Line Press, 2020) chronicles her sister's life as Clancey the Clown. Karen also co-edited, with Dr. Sally Z. Hare, *The Story Mandala: Finding Wholeness in a Divided World.*

A member of the North Carolina Poetry Society and the North Carolina Writers' Network, Karen studied with Pat Riviere-Seel in the 2018 Gilbert-Chappell Distinguished Poet Series. She holds a doctorate in education and is a facilitator with the Center for Courage & Renewal. Living in a cottage on a goat pasture in the Blue Ridge Mountains and being a grandmother are two of her greatest joys. When she's not writing, Karen companions people on their spiritual journeys. For more information, visit karenlukejackson.com.

Made in the USA
Columbia, SC
25 May 2021